Copyright © 2018 by Gwen Kruger

All rights reserved, including the right to reproduce this book or portions thereof in any form whatsoever. For information contact gwenkruger@ourhill.org

Available for purchase either paperback or digitally through Amazon

Author is available for appearances. Please e-mail through gwenkruger@ourhill.org

Website: http://www.gwenkruger.com

Illustrations by Gwen Kruger

Text by Gwen Kruger

Cover illustration Gwen Kruger

Formatting by Ken Kruger.

Manufactured in the United States of America

10 9 8 7 6 5 4 3 2 1

Kruger, Gwen

Lilly Lays An Egg: a Children's picture book/ Gwen Kruger

Paperback.

Fantasy – Washington State – Fiction

Children's picture book, fantasy, chickens

Also available in digital form

# Lily Lays an Egg

Written and illustrated by Gwen Kruger

This is Lily that laid an egg

Near a nest made of straw.

And this is the egg,

With Lily on top,

Keeping it warm.

This is Granny that wanted an egg.

So she brought some good food,

And plenty of water,

And begged for the egg.

But Lily just sat.

This is the sun that day after day

Watched the hens play

And scratch for their food

That Granny had brought.

And Lily still sat.

And these are the hens

That whispered and clucked,

How Lily was silly.

But brought her some food
Right where she sat.

This is the moon

That shone late at night.

And these are the stars

That twinkled and winkled.

And watched as she sat.

These are the clouds

Where the sun hid his face,

While the strong winds blew,

And the cold rain poured.

But Lily still sat.

After twenty one days,

The egg cracked and broke.

Something was pecking.

Out came a chick

Peeping for food.

And then happy Lily

Snuggled her chick

And taught it to eat.

And Lily ate too

And took a long drink.

That night the moon beamed

And many stars winked.

And the baby chick slept

Under Lily's warm wing.

And Lily sat still,

And smiled in her sleep

Made in the USA
Columbia, SC
08 March 2022

57409336R00020